NEW LOOK

Holes

Henry Pluckrose
Photography by Steve Shott

Ⓟ CHILDRENS PRESS ®

CHICAGO

Let us begin
with a thought.
There are holes
everywhere.

Some
holes
are
useful –

but some are not!

2

Cyclists try to avoid
holes in their way.

3

A bucket
should not
have holes
in the bottom …

but a watering can needs tiny holes –

in order to water the flowers.

Some people dig holes
and work in them ...

and other people spend time filling holes.

A window is a
hole in a wall.
From the inside
you can look out,
and from the outside
you can look in.

You could also look through a keyhole.

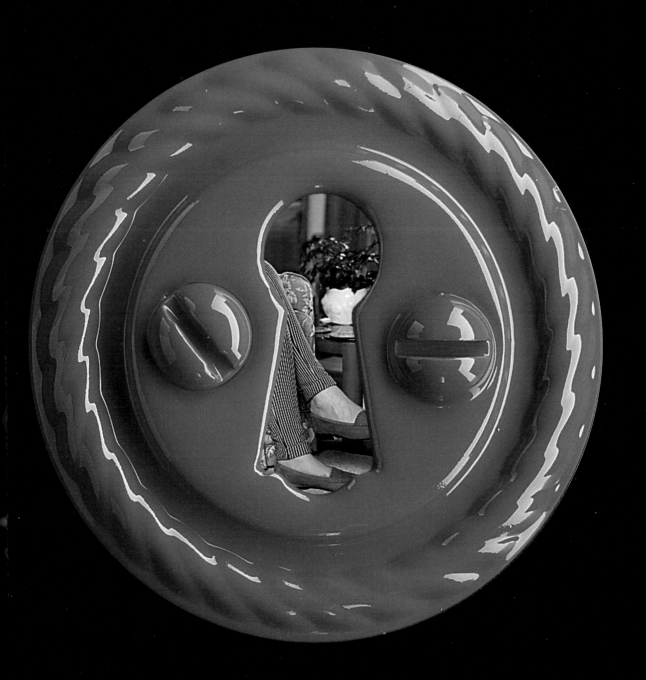

There are holes that let things out ...

and holes that let things in.

Some holes help to join things together.

A chain is made with links. Each link has a hole in it.

What fits into
this hole?

A handle is a
hole too –
a hole for
your fingers.

You use your fingers to play the flute.

The sound changes when the holes are covered — or left open.

Some holes are covered
to stop people from falling into them.

Others are covered to keep things hidden.

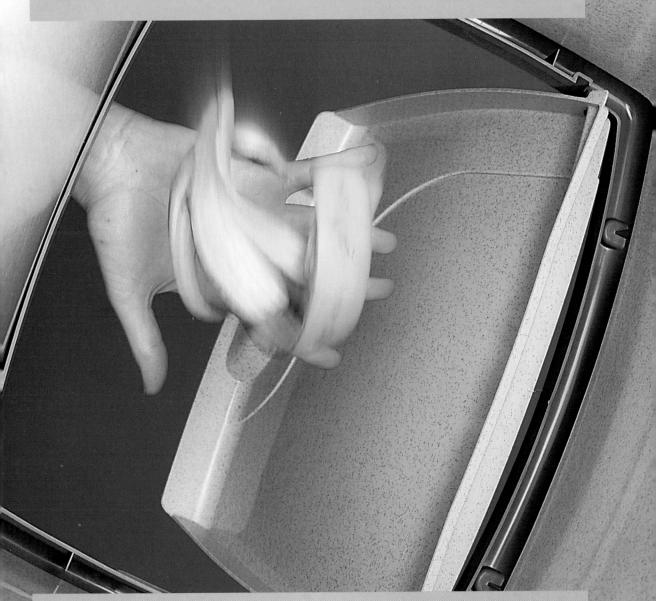

Does your garbage can have a lid?

Some holes are made in the earth.

Long holes like these are called tunnels.

A grub eats a hole through an apple.

Many animals make their homes in holes.

Some holes are there for fun!

You cannot eat the hole in a doughnut.

21

How are
holes used
in these
games?

18

What are
the holes in
these objects
used for?

Look
around you.
There are holes
everywhere.

INDEX

About this book

Children view the world from a different eye level than adults. This book, along with its companions in the **New Look** series, is a visual exploration of everyday life from the child's viewpoint. The photographs and the text encourage discussion and personal discovery — both vital elements in the learning process.

The world in which young children grow and develop is a fascinating place. New experiences — things tasted, touched, heard, smelled, and seen — crowd one upon another. Such experiences are the key to understanding, for their very richness and diversity foster curiosity and encourage questioning.

Henry Pluckrose

About the author

Henry Pluckrose is a very well-known educator and respected author of many information books for young people. He is a former primary school headmaster who is now an educational consultant for different organizations throughout the world.

Additional photographs:
Mike Davis 17

Animals supplied by:
Trevor Smith's Animal World

Editor: Annabel Martin
Design: Mike Davis

1995 Childrens Press Edition
© 1995 Watts Books, London,
New York, Sydney
All rights reserved.
Printed in Malaysia.
Published simultaneously
in Canada.
1 2 3 4 5 R 99 98 97 96 95 94

Library of Congress Cataloging-in-Publication Data

Pluckrose, Henry Arthur.
    Holes / by Henry Pluckrose: illustrated by Steve Shott.
        p. cm. — (New Look)
    ISBN 0-516-08237-X
    1. Space perception – Juvenile literature. 2. Holes – Juvenile
literature.   [1. Space perception.   2. Holes.]
    I. Shott, Stephen, ill. II. Title. III. Series.
    BF469.P58 1995   94-41102
                                                          CIP
                                                          AC

24